ínspirations

DRIED FLOWERS

Over 20 natural projects for the home

inspirations

DRIED FLOWERS

Over 20 natural projects for the home

KALLY ELLIS AND ERCOLE MORONI

PHOTOGRAPHY BY ANDREW CAMERON

LORENZ BOOKS

This edition first published in 1997 by Lorenz Books

© 1997 Anness Publishing Limited

Lorenz Books is an imprint of
Anness Publishing Limited
Hermes House
88-89 Blackfriars Road
London SE1 8HA

This edition distributed in Canada by
Raincoast Books
8680 Cambie Street
Vancouver
British Columbia V6P 6M9

ISBN 1 85967 535 2

A CIP catalogue entry for this book is available from the British Library.

Publisher: Joanna Lorenz
Senior Editor: Lindsay Porter
Designer: Ian Sandom
Photographer: Andrew Cameron
Stylist: Leeann Mackenzie

Printed in Hong Kong / China

3 5 7 9 10 8 6 4 2

CONTENTS

INTRODUCTION

FRESH FLOWERS ARE so beautiful but they do fade quickly and their beauty disappears. But don't despair, as you can have longer-lasting, colourful arrangements in your home all year round by using dried flowers.

Don't just think of dried flower arrangements as a poor relation to fresh flowers for the winter months. The colours of the flowers when they are dried are just as beautiful as the flowers when they were in their full glory in the garden. Dried petals and flower heads have been used for centuries as pot-pourri and, traditionally, dried flower arrangements have been thought of as reminiscent of Flemish still-life paintings. The extensive range of dried materials available today makes it possible to enjoy the beauty of your favourite flowers throughout the year and enables you to experiment with new textures and colours by combining flowers with interesting and unusual foliage, dried moss or even fruit, vegetables and seed pods. Each project is self-contained, and step-by-step photographs and easy-to-follow instructions illustrate every stage of preparation. Your arrangements are limited only by your imagination, and a separate reference section provides instant access to the techniques of working with dried materials and illustrates the variety of materials available.

In this book Kally Ellis and Ercole Moroni show you how to create a wide variety of displays for every room of your home and for every season. From wheatsheaf garlands and moss topiaries to an elegant table centrepiece, dried flower arrangements are the perfect way to enhance your home.

Deborah Barker

ROSE BOWL

A bowl of closely packed white roses makes a classic table centrepiece. The roses used here are white Tineke roses, but any variety or colour of dried rose would do. The idea is updated here by placing the rose heads in a diamond-shaped container to create a very contemporary look.

YOU WILL NEED
two blocks of dry florist's foam
diamond-shaped glass container
sharp knife
florist's foam fix
medium-gauge wire
lichen
approx. 50 dried white Tineke roses

1 Place two blocks of dry florist's foam side by side and place the diamond-shaped glass container centrally over them. With a sharp knife, draw a line around the container.

2 Remove the container and cut directly through the foam with the knife. Discard any excess foam. Place the diamond-shaped foam inside the glass container.

3 Secure the base of the foam with florist's foam fix. For added security, use wire pins made of short lengths of medium-gauge wire to hold the two halves of the foam together.

9

4 Fill the gap between the foam and the container with lichen. Ensure that the lichen is packed tightly, as this not only looks attractive but will act as a further anchor for the foam.

5 Prepare the roses by cutting them roughly to the same length, leaving at least 5 cm/2 in of stem. Begin to insert them into the foam, starting with the outer edge and working inwards.

6 Continue this process until the foam is completely covered, leaving no gaps in between the rose heads.

7 Ensure that all the heads are level, giving a flat, symmetrical look.

CHRISTMAS WREATH

A Christmas wreath with a difference – this one combines the rich colours of pomegranates, artichokes and chillies with the traditional elements of evergreen foliage and pine cones. This wreath may be hung on a door or placed in the centre of the dining table.

YOU WILL NEED
ball of string
copper wire wreath frame
sphagnum or carpet moss
scissors
reel wire
a bundle of blue pine branches
secateurs (pruning shears)
wire cutters
birch twigs
medium-gauge wire
freeze-dried artichokes
dried chillies
dried pomegranates
pine cones
dried lichen
glue gun and glue sticks
rope or ribbon

1 Attach the end of the ball of string to the larger outside ring of the copper frame. Begin to pad the moss to both sides of the frame evenly. Secure the moss in place by winding the string tightly around the frame as you progress. Continue this process until the whole wreath frame is evenly covered. Tie the string firmly and cut with scissors.

2 Attach the end of your reel wire to the outside ring of the frame. Snip off several sprigs of blue pine from the main branches and begin to build up a thick blue pine garland by staggering the sprigs evenly around the frame. Secure each sprig in place by winding the reel wire tightly around the stem.

3 Continue to build up the blue pine base until the whole frame is covered. The end result should be an abundant, luscious ring of foliage. Cut off the wire with wire cutters and secure tightly by twisting it around itself several times on the underside of the wreath.

4 For added interest and textural contrast, make large loops out of branches of birch twigs and place diagonally at intervals around the wreath. Secure with pins of medium-gauge wire pushed firmly through the middle of the wreath. Make these pins from short lengths of wire bent in half.

5 Prepare all your decorative materials by wiring them up individually with double-leg mount wire (see Techniques). Think carefully about your design before commencing – remember that by grouping materials you will achieve greater impact. Begin with a grouping of your largest material (the artichokes) as this will serve as your focus. Push the false stems firmly through the body of the wreath and secure by twisting the two wire prongs around one another on the underside of the wreath.

6 Wire up the chillies in threes and group them together between the artichokes in large clusters. Check which way the chillies naturally bend before deciding how to place them within the cluster.

7 Insert the pomegranates in clusters of at least five to balance the size of the artichoke and chilli groupings. Once this is complete you can begin to fill in the gaps with smaller clusters of pine cones and lichen.

8 You will need a glue gun in order to attach the lichen to the wreath. The lichen is very delicate and cannot be wired, as it will crumble. Use your own judgment as to where to place these pieces. Ensure there is an even balance all the way around. As a finishing touch, intertwine either rope or a ribbon of your choice between the groupings. Anchor this into the wreath using a length of wire folded in half to form a pin.

CHRISTMAS GARLAND

Designed to complement the Christmas wreath, this garland can be draped along a dining room mantelpiece or curled around the banister for an impressive welcome. The elements of chillies, artichokes and pomegranates will give a taste of the wonderful meal to follow.

YOU WILL NEED
ball of string
reel wire
blue pine sprigs
scissors
wire cutters
medium-gauge wire
freeze-dried artichokes
dried pomegranates
pine cones
dried chillies
rope or ribbon

1 Make a loop with the string and attach the reel wire to the base, twisting it round several times to secure. Estimate the length you wish the garland to be (ours is about 180 cm/6 ft), and cut the string accordingly. Cut your sprigs of blue pine from the main branches at roughly the same length – those with 3 prongs (shaped like a fork) are ideal for this purpose.

2 Attach your first sprig of pine over the loop and wind the reel wire around the pine and the string as tightly as possible. Add a few sprigs at a time, staggering them along the length of the string and securing with the reel wire as before.

14

3 Continue this process, remembering to alternate the sides and rotate the body of the garland to achieve a full-rounded effect. The string should be wound into the centre of the garland simultaneously to act as a core and to ensure flexibility. When you reach the end of the string, make another loop and tie with the reel wire. Cut off the reel wire with wire cutters.

4 Prepare your decorative materials by wiring them up individually using double-leg mounts made from medium-gauge wire (see Techniques). Begin inserting them into the body of the garland in clusters of three, starting with your largest-headed material – in this instance the artichoke. Space each grouping evenly along the length of the garland – approximately three in total.

5 Push the double-pronged wire stems of each item firmly through the body of the garland at a diagonal, then wind the prongs tightly round one another to secure. Place groupings of pomegranates at regular intervals between the artichoke clusters and attach to the garland using the same method.

6 To wire a pine cone, take a length of medium-gauge wire and feed between the natural "teeth" of the cone as close to the base as possible. Twist the two wire ends around one another several times and bend back to create a false stem (see Techniques). As before, insert the cones in groupings of three at regular intervals along the garland.

7 To prepare the chillies, take three at a time and wire the stalks together using double-leg mount wire (see Techniques). Introduce these into the garland in large clusters between the other main groupings.

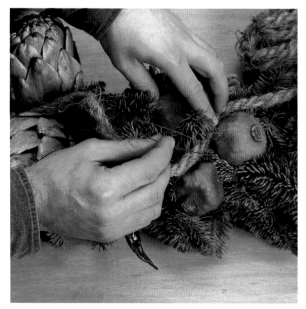

8 To finish, feed a thick, rustic rope or ribbon between the various groups. Secure it to the main body of the garland at strategic points with wire pins made of short lengths of medium-gauge wire. Do not pull the rope too tightly – a little slack looks far more natural.

WOODLAND SETTING

This is a loose and informal display and should be arranged in situ, as some of the materials are not attached with wires. To make it look as realistic as possible, try to arrange the mushrooms and fungi as they would grow naturally in the woods.

YOU WILL NEED

two blocks of dry florist's foam

plastic tray

florist's tape

medium-gauge wire

wire cutters

log night-light holders

contorted willow branches

carpet moss

catkin (pussy willow) branches

scissors or secateurs (pruning shears)

driftwood

sponge fungi

heavy-gauge wire

freeze-dried button mushrooms

night-lights

1 Place two blocks of dry foam on top of each other inside the tray. Wind the florist's tape in two positions around the foam and tray. For added security insert some wire pins made from short lengths of medium-gauge wire to join the two blocks together.

2 Prepare the log night-light holders by taping several strong wire pins around the base of each log. Push the logs firmly into the foam towards the back of the display in a solid grouping. Place the tallest log at the back with the shorter ones directly in front.

3 Insert a few contorted willow branches of varying lengths to one side of the arrangement. Push them deep into the foam to avoid movement.

4 Cover most of the foam with carpet moss, pinning it into position with wire pins. Snip off several catkin twigs and insert these around the base of the logs with a few coming over the front of the display. Position the large piece of driftwood (or any interesting piece of wood or bark) to the left of your display.

5 Select three large pieces of sponge fungi. Take a length of heavy-gauge wire and bend it in half. Pass the two prongs through the base of the fungi. Pull the wire through and twist the two ends around one another to form a strong stalk (see Techniques).

6 Introduce the sponge fungi in a bold grouping towards the front of the arrangement. Position them to appear as though they are actually growing out of the moss.

7 Prepare your button mushrooms by passing a length of medium-gauge wire about halfway through the stalks. Pull both wire ends downwards towards the stalk. There is no need to wind the wire ends around one another, as the mushroom stalks are very delicate and may get damaged. Introduce a group of the button mushrooms at the base of the logs in front of the sponge fungi. Position them to appear as though they are growing naturally from that spot.

8 Insert a night-light into the top of each log. Check the arrangement for any obvious gaps and fill with carpet moss and catkin twigs.

TABLE CENTREPIECE

Hydrangeas dry beautifully and you only need a few flowers to create a stunning effect.
Combined here with large white roses, they make a brilliantly simple arrangement that would
look good all year round. Do not let the candle burn down too near to the dried flowers.

YOU WILL NEED
small wire urn
carpet moss
one block of dry florist's foam
sharp knife
medium-gauge wire
wire cutters
church candle
florist's tape
hydrangeas
scissors or secateurs (pruning shears)
freeze-dried roses

1 Cover the inside of the wire urn with a thin layer of carpet moss.

2 With a sharp knife, cut out a piece of dry foam. Place in the centre of the container and hold in position with wire pins made of medium–gauge wire, threaded through the urn and pushed through the foam.

3 Prepare the candle by taping several wire pins around the base of the candle to form pegs.

▶

4 Insert the candle in the centre of the foam. Holding the base of the container, press down firmly until it is secure.

5 Cover the surface of the foam with a thin layer of carpet moss and secure with wire pins. Select a few choice stems of hydrangea and cut the stalks to leave at least 5 cm/2 in. Begin to insert the heads around the base of the candle so that the heads are touching the moss.

6 Freeze-dried roses are very delicate and should be handled with care. Take a short length of medium-gauge wire and make a hook by bending the top of the wire over. Thread the wire through the centre of the rose and pull down gently, until the head of the hook is hidden within the petals and the stalk is protruding sufficiently out of the base. Place the roses between the hydrangea heads in small clusters by inserting the wire stalk firmly into the foam.

7 Move the arrangement around as you continue to insert the materials until it is fully covered. The end result should be a neat, domed shape.

LAVENDER BLUE

What could be simpler than a terracotta bowl packed with lavender? This arrangement is best viewed from above, so place it low down such as underneath a glass-topped coffee table. You can dry your own lavender from the garden or use a smaller pot if you want to keep costs down.

YOU WILL NEED
two blocks of dry florist's foam
sharp knife
weathered terracotta bowl
medium-gauge wire
wire cutters
glue gun and glue sticks
lavender
scissors

1 Place two blocks of foam side by side and, using a sharp knife, cut out a rounded shape that will fit into the container. Wire the two halves together with wire pins made of medium-gauge wire. Release some hot glue on to the underside of the foam.

2 Lift carefully and place glue-side down into the container, pressing firmly until secure. Wedge small pieces of the discarded foam around the edge for full and even coverage, and fasten into position with wire pins.

3 Prepare your lavender by separating it into small bunches. Level up the heads using the palm of one hand. Hold the stems loosely in the other hand while you are doing this.

▶

4 With scissors, cut off the bulk of the stalks leaving approximately 2.5 cm/1 in. Hold the bunch tightly in your hand to avoid movement.

5 Take a length of medium-gauge wire and tightly double-leg mount each bunch (see Techniques).

6 Insert the first bunch of wired lavender against the edge of the bowl. The lavender heads should protrude approximately 1.5 cm/½ in above the lip of the container. Place each bunch tightly against the previous one, maintaining the same level.

7 Continue to work around the container until the whole surface is covered completely.

8 Trim off any stray pieces of lavender with scissors to achieve a perfectly flat surface.

MOSS TOPIARY

*Topiary has enjoyed a revival in popularity recently, and you can create your own indoor topiary-
style arrangement using bun moss pinned on to a foam base. The finished topiary ball rests on a
nest of birch twigs curled and intertwined into shape.*

YOU WILL NEED
bun moss
medium-gauge wire
wire cutters
dry foam topiary ball
birch twigs

1 Sort out some clean pieces of bun moss and
prepare some wire pins by folding short lengths of
medium-gauge wire in half. Hold the first piece of
moss firmly against the dry foam ball and anchor in
position by pushing two or three pins directly into it.

2 Introduce each piece of moss as closely as possible
to the one before to avoid any gaps. Continue to
build up your moss ball until the whole area has been
covered. Ensure that the pins are pushed as far down
as possible into the moss.

3 Take a couple of branches of birch twig and twist
them round one another to make a thick garland.
Bend the branches over gently to make a circle and tie
the ends together with wire.

▶

4 Build up your nest of twigs by threading more birch twigs through and around the first circle. This process should be done gently, as the branches are quite brittle and may snap.

5 Carefully place the finished moss ball on to the nest to show its best side.

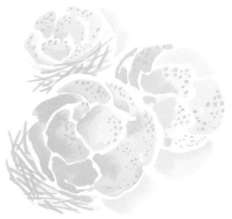

6 Check the ball for any wire pins. Should you find any, push them further down into the moss to conceal them.

MODERN LIVING

This unusual and versatile vase, known as a tse-tse vase, consists of a "snake" of tubes linked together with metal rings. The tubes can be arranged into almost any shape you like. Choose your own selection of materials to fill the tubes, such as coloured glass or sand.

YOU WILL NEED
tse-tse vase
spiral bark shavings
small bleached white stones
physalis (Chinese lantern)
glycerined eucalyptus
scissors or secateurs (pruning shears)
birch twigs

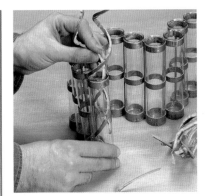

1 Ensure all the tubes are properly cleaned and dried before commencing. Insert three stems of the spiralled bark shavings into the first tube. The stems should touch the bottom of the tube for greater impact.

2 Fill the second tube with small bleached white stones. You can fill the tube right to the top or to any level, depending on personal taste.

3 In the third tube, insert a stem of physalis. These provide interest through both colour and form.

4 Insert a stem of glycerined eucalyptus into the fourth tube providing, yet again, new colour and texture to the arrangement. Cut all the stems to approximately the same height for uniformity, although this is not essential.

▶

31

5 Add a stem of birch into the fifth tube to complete the combination.

6 Continue to fill each tube, repeating the steps above until they are all full.

AUTUMN HARVEST

The rich colours of autumn are artistically combined in this rustic basket arrangement.
Reminiscent of an artist's palette, the materials are closely arranged in blocks of colour. By
keeping the stems slightly longer in the centre, the arrangement has a soft, cushioned shape.

YOU WILL NEED
rustic wire mesh basket
carpet moss
three blocks of dry florist's foam
heavy-gauge wire
wire cutters
lichen
dried orange slices
dried sunflowers
dried pomegranates
physalis (Chinese lantern)
scissors or secateurs (pruning shears)
medium-gauge wire
freeze-dried roses
dried hydrangea
sea moss

1 Cover the base of the wire mesh basket with a layer of carpet moss.
Place three blocks of foam inside the basket. Tip the basket on to its
side and pass a long length of heavy-gauge wire folded in half through the
wire mesh and into the foam until it comes through at the top. Continue
this process several times until the foam is secure.

2 Bend the ends of the wires over to form a loop and push firmly back
into the foam.

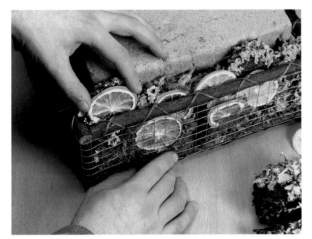

3 Fill the gaps between the sides of the basket and the foam with alternate clumps of carpet moss, lichen, orange slices and sunflower heads.

4 Prepare the pomegranates. These will be inserted into the arrangement in three groups of three – two groupings at opposite, diagonal corners and one in the centre. The pomegranates need to be wired up securely. Use two lengths of heavy-gauge wire inserted through the middle of the fruit to form a cross. Then push the four wire ends down towards the stalk and twist them round one another to create a single, solid stalk (see Techniques). Position in the basket.

5 Snip the physalis heads off the branches and wire together in clusters of three, using medium-gauge wire. Insert two clusters close together in the basket to give a solid grouping of the fruit beside the pomegranates.

6 Continue to build up the display by introducing large, solid clusters of wired roses and other materials tightly beside one another (see Techniques). The hydrangea is used here as a filler to conceal the wiring on the other materials and to cover the foam. ▶

7 The shape you are attempting to achieve is a rounded, cushion shape. Therefore, remember to leave the stems of the materials you are inserting into the centre slightly longer that those at the edge. Note how the materials at the edge are inserted at almost right angles to the basket.

8 Wire up the sea moss in small clumps using short lengths of medium-gauge wire. It is ideal to use in the gaps between the main materials. Turn the basket around as you work and check for any obvious gaps. Fill any gaps with moss or other materials.

PEONY PERFECTION

Peonies come in a wonderful range of colours from palest white to deep red. The pale pink peonies used here perfectly complement the grey cast-iron urn. Sea moss and hydrangea provide the filler materials and create the shape of the arrangement, while setting off the peonies beautifully.

YOU WILL NEED
dry florist's foam
sharp knife
cast-iron antique urn
glue gun and glue sticks (optional)
Tillandsia mosss
dried green hydrangea heads
dried peonies
scissors or secateurs (pruning shears)

1 Take two blocks of dry florist's foam and begin to shape with a sharp knife to fit snugly inside the container.

2 Place the two shaped blocks inside the container and cut away any excess. The foam should protrude approximately 2.5 cm/ 1 in above the edge of the container. You can glue the foam to the base of the container using a glue gun for added security - this should not be necessary if it is a tight fit.

▶

3 Loosely edge the rim of the container with an even, thick garland of Tillandsia moss. This will serve to conceal the foam and provide cushioning for the delicate dried flower heads.

4 Begin to cover the whole surface of the foam with large hydrangea heads. Aim to achieve a full and rounded dome shape.

5 Once the whole area is covered with hydrangea heads, begin to insert the peonies one at a time. Leave the stems of the peonies as long as possible, as this will ensure maximum anchorage. Begin with a central peony and radiate at regular intervals from this central point. The heads of the peonies should stand out slightly above the heads of the hydrangea.

6 Continue to place the peonies evenly over the surface of the arrangement until it is completely covered. Trim the stems of the peonies if necessary to create the rounded shape.

HAND-TIED POSY

Hand-tied posies have a simple, just-picked look about them, although it takes time and practice to perfect the technique of spiralling the stems to create a free-standing bouquet. The long strands of the love-lies-bleeding add rich interest to the neat, round arrangement.

YOU WILL NEED
dried hydrangea heads
dried red Europa roses
dried amaranthus (love-lies-bleeding)
dried oregano stems
scissors or secateurs (pruning shears)
raffia

1 Select your first stem of hydrangea and thread a single rose through the centre. The two stems should cross one another at diagonals.

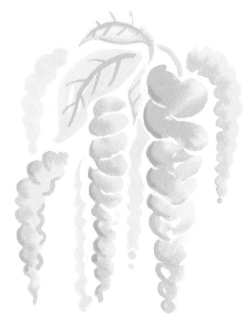

2 Begin to add the amaranthus and oregano stems symmetrically to the core, remembering to angle the stems at diagonals. This is very important to achieve the dome shape and to allow the bouquet to stand by itself once finished.

3 With one hand, continue to add further stems of each material diagonally to the bunch. Hold the bunch securely in the other hand, creating a spiralled effect as you add more material.

4 Build up the bouquet until you can no longer hold the stems comfortably in your hand. The length of the stems should be in proportion to the size of the bouquet – trim the stems accordingly to an even length.

5 Tie the bunch tightly with a piece of raffia at the narrowest part of the spiral. If the bunch is correctly made, the hand-tied bouquet should stand by itself without support.

6 Make a loose, rustic bow (see Techniques) out of several lengths of raffia and tie at the binding point. Trim off any excess or stray pieces of raffia for a neat finish.

IN THE RED

Instead of using traditional wire netting, the stems in this arrangement are anchored in wreaths of catkin (pussy willow) twigs, which look attractive viewed through the sides of the glass bowl. The rich reds of the celosia and amaranthus (love-lies-bleeding) make for an unusual combination.

YOU WILL NEED
wide-necked glass vase
catkin (pussy willow) branches
reel wire
wire cutters
scissors or secateurs (pruning shears)
dried amaranthus (love-lies-bleeding)
celosia

1 Fill the bottom of the vase with catkin twigs. Take a larger branch and bend it around itself to make a small wreath.

2 To ensure the wreath holds its shape, tie it together with lengths of reel wire. Neatly bind off the ends of the wire.

3 Make two more similar-sized wreaths using the method described, and place loosely against the sides of the vase.

4 Trim the stems of amaranthus of excess foliage and cut the stems to a length not exceeding the height of the vase itself.

5 Begin to insert the amaranthus on one side of the vase in a large cascading grouping, allowing the natural trails to hang over the edge of the vase. ▶

6 Prepare the celosia in a similar fashion by strip-ping the stems of excess foliage and cutting them down to a similar length. Begin to build up a large massed grouping of the celosia beside the amaranthus.

7 Continue to work your way around the vase, alternating the groupings of amaranthus and celosia until the whole surface has been covered.

8 The end result should be a dome-shaped, colour-blocked mound. Reposition the materials if this shape has not been achieved.

WILLOW VASE

This dramatic design is achieved with only one material – tall, contorted willow twigs arranged in a robust vase. Finished with a chunky rope, the strong, architectural shape of this arrangement would look good in a hallway or reception area.

YOU WILL NEED
large vase or urn
approx. 20 branches of contorted willow
scissors or secateurs (pruning shears)
large rope

1 Ensure the container is clean and dry. Cut all your stems of contorted willow to roughly the same length and begin to insert them into the vase. Check the way that the branches bend naturally and take this into account when planning their position.

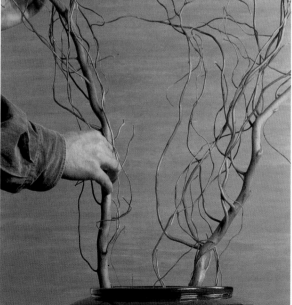

2 Continue placing one stem at a time, being careful not to damage any of the twisted twigs, which can be quite delicate. ▶

3 Shape and twist the stems around in the
container in order to get the best shape possible.

4 You will find that the more stems you introduce,
the sturdier the display is. Rearrange the stems to
achieve an even, overall shape.

5 Trim off any untidy or broken twigs with a sharp
pair of scissors or secateurs.

6 To add interest and introduce another texture,
take a thick piece of rope and tie around the top
of the vase in a loose knot. Trim to length.

ATA FRUIT URN

This urn is simply filled with a foam ball then decorated with ata fruit creating an effect similar to a giant pineapple. Like pine cones, the fruit come with stalks ready for arranging. You could choose pine cones, chestnuts or walnuts instead, but they would have to be wired first before arranging.

YOU WILL NEED
glue gun and glue sticks
antique cast-iron urn
ball of florist's foam
sea moss (or other type)
medium-gauge wire
wire cutters
ata fruit (already prepared on stalks)

1 With a glue gun, inject a line of hot glue all the way around the inside edge of the urn. Be generous with the glue to avoid any movement once the ball of foam is placed on top.

2 Place the foam ball over the urn and press down firmly. Hold for at least 30 seconds to allow the glue to set. ▶

3 Cover the surface of the foam with moss. Pin securely in place with wire pins made from short lengths of medium-gauge wire.

4 The ata fruit usually come prepared with stalks that can be inserted easily into the foam. However, for added anchorage, squeeze a drop of hot glue on to the base of the fruit before inserting it firmly into the foam.

5 Begin by placing two lines of fruit in the shape of a cross over the surface of the foam. Ensure that the heads are level with one another.

6 Fill in each quarter with more fruit. Look at the size of each fruit to see where they will be best placed, as some are smaller than others.

DAHLIA WREATH

The combination of closely packed, pale yellow dahlias looped with bleached rope makes this wreath look very springlike. It is perfect for bringing a fresh note into a bathroom, complemented by piles of fluffy, pale yellow towels.

YOU WILL NEED
reel wire
wicker wreath frame
Tillandsia moss
wire cutters
dried white dahlia heads
glue gun and glue sticks
sea-grass rope

1 Attach the end of the reel wire to the outside edge of the wreath frame and tie securely.

2 Begin to pad the wreath by adding thick layers of moss on to the top of the frame. Secure the moss tightly by winding the reel wire several times around the frame.

3 Continue to pad the moss on to the wreath frame until the whole circumference has been covered completely. Cut the reel wire and tie securely.

4 Select one dried dahlia head at a time and drop a blob of hot glue on to the underside of each. Begin to press them firmly on to the moss-covered wreath, ensuring that there are no gaps between. Overlap the flower heads if necessary.

5 Continue to press on the dahlia heads until the whole wreath has been covered. The overall result should be a padded-ring effect. Therefore, remember when gluing the heads on to the wreath to place them deep into the inner ring, and as far down to the outer edge as possible.

6 Attach sea-grass rope to the outer edge of the underside of the wreath frame. Tie in a secure knot and trim the short end.

▶

7 Begin to wind the rope loosely over the wreath, positioning it diagonally at regular intervals around the circle.

8 Turn the wreath over, underside up, and make a substantial hanging loop. Tie a secure knot quite low down where it will not be seen.

9 To finish, wind the end of the rope around the base of the loop several times in a neat spiral and tuck into the back.

LAVENDER CURTAIN

A creative alternative to bowls of scented pot-pourri is to enclose dried lavender in pockets on a voile tab-headed curtain. The curtain will catch the breeze from an open window, allowing the scent of lavender to fill the air. Add a sprig of lavender to each pocket for decoration.

YOU WILL NEED
muslin or voile fabric
tape measure
dressmaker's scissors
dressmaker's pins
iron
sewing machine
matching sewing threads
pencil
card (cardboard)
paper scissors
sewing needle
buttons
lavender pot-pourri
lavender stems
scissors
natural twine

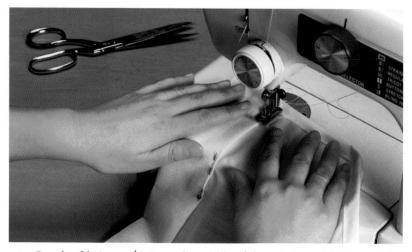

1 Cut the fabric to 1½ times the width of the window. Add 7 cm/3 in for the bottom hem and 3.5 cm/1½ in for the top hem. Fold in 1 cm/½ in, then 1 cm/½ in along both side edges. Press and pin. Turn over, making a 4 cm/1½ in double hem along the bottom and a single hem along the top. Press, pin and machine stitch both edges and hems.

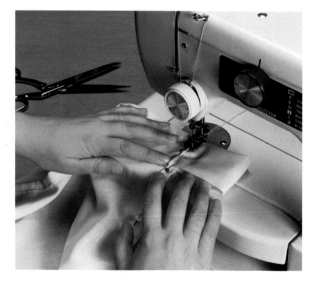

2 Prepare the loops for the top of the curtain. The loops will be positioned along the curtain at roughly 15 cm/6 in intervals. Calculate the number of loops needed and cut out a 15 cm/6 in square of fabric for each one. Fold each one in half and sew the long edges. Turn the loop inside out and iron flat with the seam in the centre. Fold each loop in half and pin to the top of the curtain, placing one at each end and the remaining loops evenly spaced in between. Fold the top edge under and sew down so that all the frayed edges are concealed.

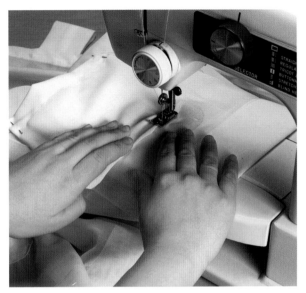

3 To prepare the pockets, make a card template to the required size. Cut the fabric slightly larger than the template leaving about 2 cm/¾ in extra all the way round, and at least 4 cm/1½ in at the top for the hem. Fold down the top edge twice by 2 cm/¾ in each time, and sew a hem.

4 Fold under the seam allowance on three sides of each pocket and press. Place the pockets on the curtain and pin in place. Sew around all edges.

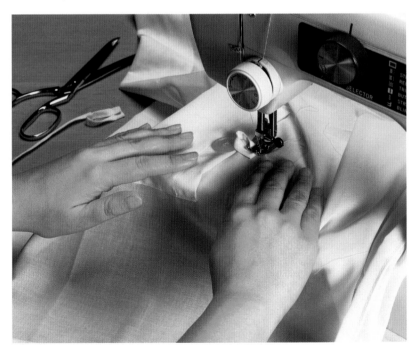

5 Sew a button to the centre top of each pocket. Prepare the rouleau loop fastenings. For each pocket you will need a 6 cm x 2 cm/2½ in x ¾ in strip of fabric. Fold the edges to meet in the middle. Fold in half again and stitch along the edge. Trim to the length required to fit over the button. Pin either side of the button and stitch in place. ▶

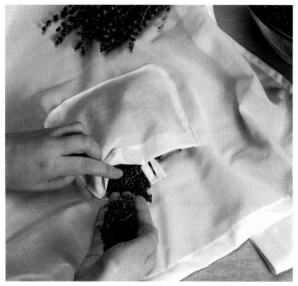

6 Half-fill each pocket with lavender pot-pourri. Take several stems of lavender, bunch them together with their heads level and cut off any excess stems. Bind with natural twine.

7 Insert the bunch of lavender to one side of the pocket so that the heads protrude at least 4 cm/1½ in over the top of the pocket. Fasten the button loop.

VEGETABLE BOX

This old-fashioned wooden cutlery drawer is ideal for this unusual kitchen arrangement. The foam blocks slot snugly into the compartments, giving it a good, solid base. Be careful when handling the spring onions (scallions) and mushrooms as they bruise easily.

YOU WILL NEED
two blocks of dry florist's foam
sharp knife
old wooden box
carpet moss
medium-gauge wire
wire cutters
freeze-dried artichokes
heavy-gauge wire
freeze-dried spring onions (scallions)
raffia ribbon
scissors
freeze-dried button mushrooms

1 Trim the blocks of foam with a sharp knife to fit snugly inside the two halves of the box.

2 Cover the whole surface of the box with carpet moss, leaving only the handle free. Secure the moss into position, using wire pins made from medium-gauge wire.

3 The artichokes are a weighty material and should be wired up using heavy-gauge wire. You will need two lengths of wire inserted through the base of each artichoke to form a cross (see Techniques).

4 Bend all four wire ends down towards the stems of the vegetable and wrap one end around the remaining three to create a strong stalk.

5 You will need six artichokes in total to create two groupings of three. These should be placed at opposite corners of the box in a diagonal line.

6 Prepare three bunches of spring onions by taking several stems and wiring them together in the middle using a length of medium-gauge wire (see Techniques).

7 Conceal the wire by tying a raffia ribbon over the binding point, leaving the two ends of wire free to insert into the moss and foam. Position the bunches of spring onions around the outer edge of the box with their heads pointing downwards and green stalks upwards.

▶

8 Introduce the mushrooms in large clusters between the artichokes. Prepare them by threading a length of medium-gauge wire through the stalks and bending the two ends downwards (see Techniques). Do not wind the ends around one another as the mushrooms are a very soft and delicate material and are easily damaged.

9 Push the mushrooms gently into the moss and foam, and position them to appear as though they are growing naturally.

MINI-CORN RIDDLE

Dried corn-on-the-cob are popular in America as Thanksgiving decorations, but they make an attractive kitchen display at any time of year. The cobs come in a range of hues from pale yellow to rich orange. Hop garlands and an old wooden riddle add to the charm of this rustic display.

YOU WILL NEED
medium-gauge wire
wire cutters
wooden riddle frame
hop garland
scissors or secateurs (pruning shears)
mini corn-on-the-cob

1 Thread a length of medium-gauge wire through the existing hole of the wooden riddle frame and around the wire mesh. Repeat on all four sections of the riddle where there is an existing hole.

2 Cut four short lengths of hop garland and attach the ends to the wires on the riddle frame. Twist the wire ends several times around one another until the garland is secure. Continue in this manner until the whole edge has been loosely covered.

3 Choose three corn heads of similar length and begin to tie them together with a separate length of medium-gauge wire. Holding the cluster of corn tightly together with one hand, fold the wire over the leaves of all three cobs. Twist the wire ends around one another until secure.

4 To conceal the wire, fold down a few of the dried corn leaves and wrap these around the wire.

▶

5 Tie the ends of the leaves with another length of wire to form a tuft. Trim any excess wires and leaves where necessary.

6 Begin to attach the groups of corn around the riddle frame by threading the wire legs through the mesh and on to the hop garland. Twist the wire ends around one another securely. The groups of corn should be staggered at regular intervals around the riddle frame.

7 Trim off any excess wires and corn leaves. Do not overtrim as this will detract from the natural rustic charm of the arrangement.

8 Once all the groups are attached, they can be manoeuvred easily. Do not be afraid to vary the direction in which they are pointing to achieve the most natural appearance.

HOT CHILLIES

Like spurting hot flames, chilli peppers make a fiery display. A thick, white church candle makes a cool contrast to the rich red. A galvanized flowerpot is a simple choice of container, but traditional terracotta would look just as good and be in keeping with the natural style.

YOU WILL NEED
dry florist's foam
sharp knife
galvanized flowerpot
carpet moss
thick church candle
florist's tape
medium-gauge wire
wire cutters
dried chillies

1 Take a block of dry florist's foam and use a sharp knife to shape the foam to fit comfortably inside the flowerpot. It is useful to have the container standing nearby while you carry out this process.

2 The foam should stand at least 2 cm/¾ in above the rim of the container. Wedge the foam into position with small offcuts of excess foam.

3 Fill in the gaps between the container and the foam with carpet moss. Pack the moss as tightly as possible to avoid movement.

4 Slice off any excess foam along the top using a sharp knife.

5 Take a large church candle and prepare it by taping several wire pins, made from lengths of medium-gauge wire, around the base.

6 Hold the candle firmly in both hands and push the pins directly and centrally into the foam until it is secure.

7 Cover the area between the candle and the edge of the container with carpet moss to create a mound. Secure in position with wire pins.

8 Prepare your chillies by wiring them into groupings of three. Use the double-leg mount technique (see Techniques).

9 Before inserting the bunches of chilli into the moss and foam, look carefully at the way the chillies naturally bend before deciding at which angle they should be positioned. Begin to build up a garland of chillies neatly and compactly around the base of the candle.

10 Complete the chilli garland, readjusting the position of the bunches if necessary.

WHEATSHEAF GARLAND

If you have a country-style kitchen, then this wheatsheaf garland would be the perfect decoration. It would also look good as the centrepiece of a harvest festival display and could be kept from year to year. Prepare plenty of bunches of wheat in advance to speed up the assembly time.

YOU WILL NEED
several bunches of wheat
ball of string
scissors
thick rope
heavy-gauge wire
wire cutters

1 Strip all the wheat stems of any excess foliage and begin to put them into small bunches with the heads as level as possible.

2 Wind the string several times around the stems as close to the heads as possible. Tie in a secure knot and trim the ends.

3 Trim the stems, leaving approximately 10 cm/4 in. Make up several small bunches before you start building up the garland.

4 Attach the ball of string to the first bunch and place the second diagonally across the first. Wrap the string several times around both bunches.

5 Continue to place each bunch diagonally to the one before. It is this procedure which gives the garland its spiralled effect.

▶

6 Once you have achieved the required length, tie a knot with the string and cut. Take the thick rope and wire it to the top of the garland as deep into the spiral as possible to conceal the wire.

7 Gently wind the rope through the spiral gaps as neatly as possible. The rope should fit snugly into the crevices to camouflage the string ties.

8 When you reach the bottom of the garland, make a large loop out of the rope and tie the string several times around the wheat and the rope to hold it in position.

9 Wind the excess rope neatly around the wheat ends in a spiral, pulling it as tightly as possible to avoid movement.

10 Cut a length of heavy-gauge wire and secure the end of the rope by threading the wire through the body of the garland and twisting it back and around itself.

FRUIT GARLAND

Raid the pantry and scrap box, add garden clippings and dried fruit slices and you have all the
ingredients for a delightful garland to hang in the kitchen window.

YOU WILL NEED
medium-gauge wire
wire cutters
bundle of twigs
gilt wax polish
dried bay leaves
dried pear slices
fabric scraps
dried apple slices
dried orange slices
small rubber bands
cinnamon sticks
gold twine
beeswax candle ends

1 Wire together bundles of twigs, then gild them by rubbing in gilt wax polish.

2 Make up the fruit bundles. Make a small loop at one end of a length of medium-gauge wire. Thread on some dried bay leaves, and then a dried pear, passing the wire through the rind at the top and bottom. Make a hook at the top. ▶

3 Tie a scrap of coloured fabric to the bottom loop and a scrap of green at the top, to look like leaves. Make the apple slice bundles by threading on several apple slices followed by the bay leaves.

4 Wire up pairs of thinner sliced apples by passing a wire through the centre and twisting the wires together at the top. Wire up orange slices in the same way.

5 Use small rubber bands to make up bundles of cinnamon sticks.

6 String the elements together using gold twine, knotting beeswax candle ends in at intervals.

FRUIT TOPIARY

Strawberries and raspberries do not grow together, nor do they grow on trees. However, you can create your own fantasy fruit trees with freeze-dried fruits and a little imagination. Why not make a pair of matching trees to flank a door or to adorn a mantelpiece?

YOU WILL NEED
dry florist's foam
sharp knife
rustic basket
medium-gauge wire
wire cutters
glue gun and glue sticks
dry foam topiary pyramid
Tillandsia moss
heavy-gauge wire
lichen
freeze-dried strawberries
freeze-dried raspberries

1 Take the block of dry florist's foam and trim it with a sharp knife to fit snugly inside your basket. Should you require two pieces, secure these together with pins made from short lengths of medium-gauge wire. For added security, you can glue the base of the foam to the basket itself using a glue gun.

2 Take the foam pyramid and cover it completely with Tillandsia moss, fastened with small wire pins. Trim off any stray pieces of moss to maintain a neat pyramid shape.

3 Place the pyramid centrally over the top of the basket and secure using long, heavy-gauge wire pins pushed diagonally through the base of the pyramid and into the foam below. Use as many as necessary until you feel confident that the structure will hold in position.

4 Using a glue gun, begin to stick small pieces of lichen randomly over the pyramid. This material is introduced to add new texture and to give the display a frosted look. The lichen is very delicate and should be handled gently.

5 Using a sharp knife, cut the strawberries in half and begin to glue to the pyramid structure at regular intervals. Hold the strawberry firmly against the pyramid until the glue has dried. ▶

6 Glue on clusters of raspberries between the strawberry halves wherever necessary to ensure even coverage.

FLORIST'S EQUIPMENT

DRIED FOAM
This material is sturdier than foam used for fresh flowers as it does not need to absorb any water. The foam can be cut to the size required with a sharp knife.

FLORIST'S TAPE
This is useful to hold dried florist's foam firmly in its container.

GLUE GUN AND GLUE STICKS
A glue gun will heat glue, allowing it to be applied accurately in small blobs. Once the glue has been applied, hold the item in place for a few seconds to allow the glue to set. This glue has a strong holding power.

GUTTA PERCHA TAPE
Use for wrapping round false wire stems (see Techniques).

SCISSORS
Use a good, sharp pair of scissors for cutting twine or ribbon. A separate pair can be used for cutting the stems of some natural materials as well as reel wire.

SECATEURS (PRUNING SHEARS)
Use for natural materials with woody stems or for other flowers. Secateurs can be used to cut fine wire, but will become blunt if used on thicker gauges of wire.

SHARP KNIFE
A sharp knife is invaluable for cutting dried florist's foam to size as well as for cutting woody stems of natural materials. Keep knives in good condition and cut away from yourself to avoid injury.

SPRAY PAINTS
Working in a well-ventilated area, spray the object from the distance recommended by the manufacturer. Apply a thin, even mist of paint to the surface.

STRING
Natural string is used to bind materials into garlands or for hand-tied posies.

WIRE
Different gauges of wire are useful for holding and wiring different weights of material. Reel wire is very fine and can be cut with scissors. Use this for binding twigs and branches in place on garlands or wreaths. Medium-gauge wire can be cut into shorter lengths to make "pins" for securing dried florist's foam into containers.

WIRE CUTTERS
Medium- and heavy-gauge wire should be cut with wire cutters.

Opposite: Top row, from left to right: scissors, wire cutters (pruning shears), glue gun and glue stick, spray paint, dried foam cone. Middle row, from left to right: sharp knife, medium- and heavy-gauge wires in different lengths, dried foam sphere. Bottom row, from left to right: natural string, reel wire, florist's tape, gutta percha tape, dried foam block.

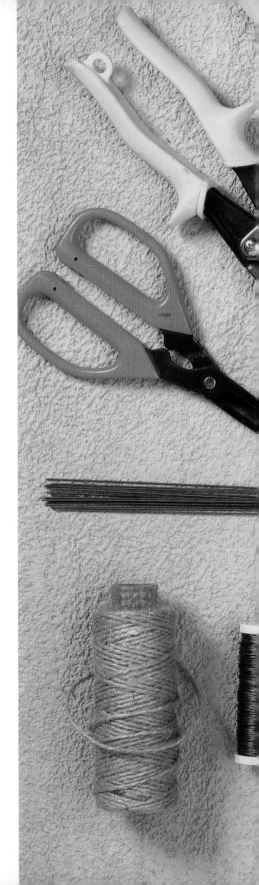

DRIED FLOWERS

Today, there is more dried material available than ever before. You can dry your own material at home, using glycerine or desiccants (see Techniques), or you can dry material by simply air-drying.

If you want something very special, however, and do not wish to wait for your own materials to dry, many florists stock an increasingly wide range of beautiful natural materials and will be able to offer advice on combining colours and textures. If you require a large amount of a particular flower, they may even be able to order your materials specially.

When drying your own flowers, the object is to achieve a look of dried fresh flowers, not desiccated dead ones. To do this, remember that you need to remove the moisture from the flower or other plant material as quickly as possible. Air-drying is the simplest form of flower preservation, requiring no specialist materials or expertise. Moisture is removed from the petals simply by circulating air. Ensure that the flowers are dry with no residual moisture from rain or dew. Choose perfect specimens only, as imperfections look unsightly in preserved arrangements. Remove any large leaves as they become shrivelled and unattractive when dried. Smaller leaves can be removed by rubbing them off before drying.

Flowers may be dried by hanging them upside-down in a dark, airy place. Gather the stems into small bunches – if they are too large they will rot. Fasten each bunch with elastic bands, which will contract as the stems dry and shrink. Hydrangeas respond well to an alternative method of drying. You must have fully mature stems, otherwise the flowers will shrivel and curl. Place the hydrangea stems in a container with 2.5 cm/ 1 in of water and allow them to take up the water and then dry out.

Opposite: Dried materials in a wealth of beautiful colours include hydrangeas (1), peonies (2), lavender (3), physalis (Chinese lanterns) (4), wheat (5), roses in all colours (6, 8, 10, 14, 15), sunflowers (7), dahlias (9, 12), amaranthus (love-lies-bleeding) (11), and celosia (13).

ADDITIONAL DRIED MATERIAL

Choose your foliage and mosses as carefully as you would your main flowers – they are, of course, wonderful filler material, setting off the main focal flowers beautifully, but the range of colours and possibilities for textural interest should not be over-looked. There are so many different varieties of foliage and mosses available today in varying neutral and colourful shades; each offers something different.

You can create stunning arrangements solely based around foliage: try using beech leaf branches punctu-ated with golds and splashes of copper to create a deeply coloured display. Or use the silvery-grey variety of eucalyptus with pale greens to create a light, airy arrangement. Try birch twigs as part of a wood-land display or blue pine sprigs when making Christmas wreaths. Contorted willow is good when used in arrangements for its oriental appearance and looks best when massed together on its own.

The texture of the moss you choose will create different effects. It is perfect for lining a container or hiding the wire fixings that will support the structure of your arrangement. Of the many varieties of mosses that are available, the following are easy to obtain and very versatile: sea moss, bun moss, sphagnum moss, lichen and carpet moss. Bun moss is particularly appealing because of its rounded form and velvety texture. The silver-encrusted appearance of lichen makes it very versatile in floral arrangements. It has the effect of bringing other colours to the fore and adding an unusual dimension to the display.

Using wood and organic materials gives an arrangement a natural, earthy appeal. Tree bark comes in a variety of shapes and sizes and should be selected accordingly. Flat bark is deliberately square- or rectangle-shaped and is ideal for lining square glass vases or wire baskets. Driftwood can also form the integral part of an organic display. Sponge mushrooms can work well when introduced in clusters at the edges of an arrangement, and golden mushrooms also work best in clusters or when arranged in delicate work such as wreath decorations. For autumn and winter arrangements, try adding pine cones and cinnamon sticks. For something a little more unusual, use lotus pods to fill large gaps or try adding panchu spring, an exotic-looking woody stem, to add interest to vase arrangements.

Opposite: Sea moss (1), birch (2), Tillandsia moss (3), sphagnum moss (4), blue pine (5), carpet moss (6), glycerined copper beech (7), cocco fibre (8), lichen (9), glycerined eucalyptus (10), bun moss (11), contorted willow (12).

Left: Flat bark (1), sponge mushrooms (2), panchu spring (3) tree bark (4), pine cones (5), driftwood (6), cinnamon sticks (7), golden mush-rooms (8), lotus pods (9).

TECHNIQUES

More dried materials are available to buy than ever before, but many plants can be dried
successfully at home. Unless a plant comes with a natural stem for arranging, you need to create a
false stem, using wire. This enables you to insert the different materials into the foam base.
Practise the techniques on old dried flowers you have at home before trying them out on new
material bought specifically for an arrangement.

PRESERVING FOLIAGE IN GLYCERINE

1 Choose a container large enough to take the foliage and add the glycerine.

2 Top this up with 2 parts hot water to 1 part glycerine to a depth of 8 cm/3 in. Mix well.

3 For wood-stemmed foliage, cut and split the stem ends, then place in the glycerine mixture imme-
diately. For calyces, seed heads, herbaceous foliage and soft-stemmed leaves, allow the mixture to cool first. Stand the container in a warm, dry, dark place.

4 Check the container every day and top up with fresh glycerine mixture if necessary. You will notice the foliage changing colour as the glycerine is gradually absorbed. Wipe the stems dry the moment they are removed from the mixture. If the leaves have absorbed too much glycerine they will look oily and will be prone to mildew. If they have been over-glycerined, immerse the foliage in warm water with a drop of washing-up liquid, rinse, shake off excess water and stand in a warm place to dry.

DRYING WITH DESICCANT

1 Spoon a layer of silica gel or borax into a container to a depth of 1 cm/½ in. For silica gel, use an airtight container. Preserve one layer of flowers per container to avoid damaging them.

2 Continue sprinkling the material so the crystals gradually cover the flower. Continue so there is a 1 cm/½ in layer on top of the flower.

3 If using silica gel, cover the container with a lid or with kitchen foil sealed with tape to make it airtight. Label with the plant name and date. If using borax, do not seal the container, but leave in a warm place with a constant temperature, such as an airing cupboard. As a rough guide, miniature flowers may take 3-4 days to dry, roses 7-10 days and fleshy flowers such as orchids 2-3 weeks. To test the flowers, gently scrape back the desiccant and remove a single flower. If it looks dry, flick it gently with your finger. If it makes a crisp, papery sound it is dry. Pour off the desiccant, catching each flower as you do.

SINGLE-LEG MOUNT

1 Small blooms will not need as much strength to support them as heavier materials. Cut off the stem at the flower head, leaving just a short length. Insert a wire through the remaining stem. Insert the wire up through the stem, right into the flower. Form a hook and pull back down, embedding the hook in the flower-head.

2 Bind this false stem with florist's tape. Hold the tape at the top of the flower head and pull down as you bind. Work to the end of the wire and finish off neatly.

DOUBLE-LEG MOUNT

1 This technique can be used on either a single stem as reinforcement, or to group several smaller stems together to form a solid bunch. Hold your material tightly in one hand directly below the flower head. Place a length of wire centrally behind the stems, and draw both ends of the wire downwards towards the stalks.

2 Twist one end of the wire tightly around the flower stems and the other end in a spiral. Trim the wire ends to the same length.

WIRING HEAVY FRUIT OR VEGETABLES

1 Heavy materials require extra support, so you should use heavy-gauge wire for their preparation. Take a length of wire and pass it directly through the base of the material until it appears on the other side. The two ends of the wire should be roughly the same length.

2 Turn your material around and do the same with a second length of wire to form a cross.

3 Push all four ends of wire down towards the stalk until they are vertical.

4 Take one of the wire ends, and wind it in a spiral around the stalk of your material and the other three wire ends to achieve a sturdy, false stem.

WIRING CONES

1 Depending on the size and weight of the cone, take a length of heavy- or medium-gauge wire and begin to thread around the base of cone between the "teeth" of the cone.

2 Once you have worked all the way round, twist the two wire ends tightly around one another to form a "stem".

WIRING SPONGE FUNGI

1 The base of the sponge fungi is very hard. You will need a craft knife to make two holes through which to thread your wire.

2 Take a length of heavy-gauge wire and bend in half. Pass each wire end through the two holes created with the craft knife. Pull the two ends down all the way and twist one end tightly around the other.

WIRING BUNCHES OF SPRING ONIONS

1 Take a few stems of spring onions and hold tightly together in one hand. Place a length of medium-gauge wire horizontally over the point where you wish to bind.

2 Bend the two ends of wire vertically downwards and twist one around the other until the vegetables are held together firmly.

3 To conceal the wire, wrap a few strings of raffia around it and tie a neat knot.

TO MAKE A BOW

1 To make a two-looped bow, start by selecting a length of ribbon. Make sure the ribbon is long enough to accommodate the size of loop required. Bend the end over itself at a diagonal and pinch together where it crosses.

2 Fold the other end over to form a figure-of-eight and pinch at the centre in the same place.

3 Continue to make a further two loops of the same size by pinching the ribbon in the centre for each. Hold the pinched parts tightly between your thumb and forefinger to avoid movement. Both halves of the bow should comprise two loops. With a pair of sharp scissors, snip the end of the ribbon at an angle after the last loop.

4 Still holding the bow tightly between the thumb and forefinger, take a piece of the same ribbon and place it over the middle of the bow at the point where all the loops meet. Tie the short piece of ribbon tightly around the middle of the bow and adjust the loops so that the bow is rounded and symmetrical. Trim off any excess ribbon using a pair of sharp scissors and snipping at an angle

STOCKISTS

UNITED KINGDOM
David Adam Sales Co.
Freelands House
33 Freelands Road
Bromley
Kent BR1 3HZ
Tel: (0181) 313 3445
Fax: (0181) 402 2244

Floralco Limited
Clapton Revel
Falcons Croft
Wooburn Moor
Bucks HP10 0NH
Tel/fax: (01628) 810412

The Hop Shop
Castle Farm
Shoreham
Sevenoaks, Kent
Tel: (01959) 523919

Machin & Henry International Ltd
Unit 103, Building A
Faircharm Trading Estate
Creekside
London SE8 3DX
Tel: (0181) 692 0227
Fax: (0181) 692 5449

Robson Watley International
2A Pembroke Road
Bromley, Kent BR1 2RU
Tel: (0181) 466 0830
Fax: (0181) 466 0831

Ruckley Dried Flowers
Shifnal
Shropshire TF11 8PQ
Tel: (01952) 460427
Fax: (01952) 462780

UNITED STATES
Dody Lyness Co.
7336 Berry Hill Drive
Polos Verdes Peninsula, CA 90274
Tel: (310) 377 7040

Gailann's Floral Catalog
821 W. Atlantic Street
Branson, MO 65616

Nature's Finest
PO Box 10311, Dept. CSS
Burke, VA 22009

Val's Naturals
PO Box 832
Kathleen, FL 33849
Tel: (813) 858 8991

AUSTRALIA
Hedgerow Flowers
177 King William Road
Hyde Park, SA 5061
Tel: (03) 9596 8742

Yuulong Lavender Estate
Yendon Road, Mt Egerton
Vic 3352
Tel: (053) 689 453

CANADA
Crafts Canada
440-28 Street, NE, Calgary
Alberta T2A 6T3
Tel: (403) 569 2355

Multi-Crafts and Gifts
2210 Thurston Drive, Ottawa
Ontario K1G 5L5

ACKNOWLEDGEMENTS

The author and publishers would like to thank Tim Birks, Eliza Wheatley, Sue Hingston, Mark Todd, Nicola Lewis, Delia Kendall, Clare Teng, Damien Kelleher and John Tibble. Special thanks to Antonia Jack for the Lavender Curtain, and Rene Mackor for supplying all dried materials. The Fruit Garland on pages 75-77 was designed by Tessa Evelegh and photographed by Michelle Garrett

INDEX